SONG 1: An introvert mu
function in the world.

SONG 2: The first person to live on Mars tells those on Earth what it's like there.

SONG 3: Facebook and Twitter run for presidency in the next election.

SONG 4: Happiness has to be summarized for somebody who has never experienced it.

_____

_____

_____

_____

_____

_____

_____

_____

_____

_____

_____

_____

_____

_____

_____

_____

_____

_____

_____

_____

_____

_____

_____

SONG 5: A meat eater and a vegan attempt to convince each other of their beliefs.

_____

_____

_____

_____

_____

_____

_____

_____

_____

_____

_____

_____

_____

_____

_____

_____

_____

_____

_____

_____

_____

SONG 6: Humans can no longer hear smartphone notifications.

SONG 7: Doctors line up in the waiting room, awaiting a certain patient to invite them in.

_____

_____

_____

_____

_____

_____

_____

_____

_____

_____

_____

_____

_____

_____

_____

_____

_____

_____

_____

SONG 8: An investment banker wants to prove that
money can actually buy love.

SONG 9: If a pet cat could speak and convey what their owner means to them.

SONG 10: The world's supply of chocolate disappears overnight.

SONG 11: A student can only re-sit their exam one more time before they get kicked out of college.

SONG 12: A group of rebellious teddy bears go on attack.

SONG 13: The sun becomes too hot to be outside for more than five minutes at a time.

_____

_____

_____

_____

_____

_____

_____

_____

_____

_____

_____

_____

_____

_____

_____

_____

_____

_____

_____

SONG 14: Aliens take charge of the American government.

SONG 15: A serial killer listens to classical music before committing their next crime.

SONG 16: A captain must take his long-loved ship to the scrapyard.

SONG 17: The strongest emotion that can be felt must be described in a short speech.

_____

_____

_____

_____

_____

_____

_____

_____

_____

_____

_____

_____

_____

_____

_____

_____

_____

_____

_____

SONG 18: The clouds in the sky have turned into giant marshmallows.

SONG 19: A police officer must arrest the man she is in love with.

SONG 20: A global warning is given that the world population must not exceed ten billion.

SONG 21: Two lovers try to make it work despite opposing political views.

_____

_____

_____

_____

_____

_____

_____

_____

_____

_____

_____

_____

_____

_____

_____

_____

_____

_____

_____

_____

_____

SONG 22: An impromptu dodgeball game takes place in an airport.

_____

_____

_____

_____

_____

_____

_____

_____

_____

_____

_____

_____

_____

_____

_____

_____

_____

_____

SONG 23: A husband and wife put super glue on their lips before their next kiss.

SONG 24: The 'H' in the HOLLYWOOD sign goes missing, and is found somewhere peculiar.

SONG 25: A native American and African tribesman tell each other about their cultures.

SONG 26: People suddenly look forward to Mondays more than any other day of the week.

SONG 27: A dog owner goes to the park every morning, but there is no dog on the lead.

SONG 28: It goes dark at midday with no explanation.

SONG 29: A school puts a ban on all forms of social media.

SONG 30: The Mona Lisa painting is on the wall of every home around the world.

SONG 31: Jealousy no longer exists.

SONG 32: Three cars break down on the same street in one night.

SONG 33: A rainbow has remained over the city for the past month.

SONG 34: The perfect sandwich has been created for all
to enjoy.

SONG 35: A mental health inpatient is told she is free to leave after four years in recovery.

SONG 36: Memories cannot be stored for more than forty-eight hours.

SONG 37: A public service announcer must cheer up hoards of depressed commuters.

_____

_____

_____

_____

_____

_____

_____

_____

_____

_____

_____

_____

_____

_____

_____

_____

_____

_____

_____

SONG 38: An elderly man takes the same trip every year to visit a cherry blossom tree in Japan.

SONG 39: A gymnast jumps and flips her way through a traffic jam.

SONG 40: The sea turns green and trees turn blue.

SONG 41: A business executive cannot stop checking her inbox for life-changing news.

SONG 42: An insomniac is losing touch with reality.

SONG 43: A prisoner gets what they wish for, just for one day.

SONG 44: Starbucks add a new mysterious ingredient to their coffee.

SONG 45: A lawyer wants to rid society of criminals altogether.

SONG 46: A pilot wants to give his passengers the best
flight of their lives.

SONG 47: McDonalds employees lock their doors in fear.

SONG 48: A dictator is now in power and they have a devilish plan.

SONG 49: No one is surprised by anything anymore.

SONG 50: A pianist and guitarist couple break-up but resolve to keep making music together.

Made in the USA
Monee, IL
15 April 2025

15865085R00059